THE GALE & POLDEN TRAINING SERIES

INTELLIGENCE *and* LIAISON

By
COLONEL G A WADE, M.C.

AUTHOR OF
" The Defence of Bloodford Village," etc.

The Naval & Military Press Ltd

Published by

The Naval & Military Press Ltd
Unit 5 Riverside, Brambleside
Bellbrook Industrial Estate
Uckfield, East Sussex
TN22 1QQ England

Tel: +44 (0)1825 749494

www.naval-military-press.com
www.nmarchive.com

In reprinting in facsimile from the original, any imperfections are inevitably reproduced and the quality may fall short of modern type and cartographic standards.

SUMMARY

INTELLIGENCE AND LIAISON.
Sometimes confused.
Inter = between. Legere = to choose.
"Liaison" is a French word.
Both have Common Object.
War against arch-enemy of all operations.

THE FOG OF WAR.
Unenviable job of commander.
Must decide and act on scanty information.

THE INTELLIGENCE OFFICER.
Revel in work.
Patron Saint, Nosey Parker.
Able to separate information.
Imagination—soldierly and systematic habits.
F.S. Regs.: "Basis of all military plans good information."
I.O. must collect, sort, check, register and
Present accurately to C.O.

COLLECTION OF INFORMATION.
Some I.Os. draw it like a magnet.

SOURCES OF INFORMATION.
Plate 1. (Detail various sources.)
Help may come unexpectedly from any one of them.
Own unit—Scouts—Patrols—Observers, etc.
Negative reports of value.
"Tiny fragments pieced together."
Training of personnel in "normal" times.
Manning of O.Ps.—quick communication.
Intelligence Section: 1 officer, 4 other ranks.
Sometimes necessary to send out own scouts.
Visits to Higher Formations, etc.

LEARN TO SPOT IMPORTANT POINTS.
Vital Point in a flood of information.
Clapping of hands.
"Balees" who barricaded themselves in.

HOT OR COLD?
Information going cold all the time.
Look out for "dawdlers."

WHAT I.O. WANTS TO KNOW ABOUT ENEMY (Plate 4).
Enemy's order of battle.
Armament—equipment—distribution.
His organization—strength—morale.
Plan of attack or defence.
New tactics, new weapons.
Where are his guns?
Information about tactical features.
Food and ammunition situation.

PRESENTING THE PICTURE.
Sort out important matters.
Look out for gaps.
Initiate steps to obtain missing items.
Pass to Adjutant or C.O.
Without expression of opinion.
C.O. wants **facts, not opinions.**
Keep other formations and units posted with news.
Prepare list.

THE CALM BEFORE THE STORM.
Lot of spadework required before battle.
Lectures and exercises to improve **Observation** and **Reporting.**
Aim to practise every officer and man.
Give lead as to **kind of information wanted.**
Training of Intelligence Section—team work.
Good filing and record system.
Plate 2: Describe Battalion Battle H.Q.
Plate 3: Describe Battle Boards.
Supply of **maps.**
All members of Intelligence Section should do I.O.'s work.
Use of Intelligence Section in operations.
" Buildings which have views."
Position of telephones.
Divide battalion area into four parts.

I.O. HAS A HEAVY JOB.
Also expected to know about own troops.
Security arrangements—Careless talk.
Disposition of neighbouring units.

SECRET ARRANGEMENTS.
In case enemy occupies area.

A JOB WHICH CALLS FOR HARD WORK.
A stout **heart** and **brains.**

IT IS A RESPONSIBILITY ANY MAN MAY BE EXTREMELY PROUD TO CARRY.

THE LIAISON OFFICER

LIAISON OFFICER.
>Different from I.O.
>L.O. should know I.O.'s job.
>Liaison Officers very fashionable nowadays.
>Must be men of ability.

HOW TO BEGIN.
>What information will be required?
>Mayor—Police—A.R.P. Controller.
>Get military knowledge **before** operations start.
>C.O. will say how much can be passed on.
>" Clear, sharply focused picture or blurred image? "

WHAT THE CIVIL AUTHORITIES WANT TO KNOW.
>1. Military dispositions.
>2. Position of field ambulances, etc.
>3. Intention of Military Commander.
>4. General situation.
>5. Progress of fighting (if any).

DO NOT VOLUNTEER INFORMATION UNNECESSARILY.

PERIODIC VISITS TO YOUR UNIT.

YOUR C.O. MAY WISH TO KNOW:
>1. State of civil morale.
>2. Blitz damage.
>3. Likelihood of refugee troubles.
>4. Whereabouts and capacity of decontamination.
>5. Number of ambulances available.
>6. Number of buses in running order.
>7. Food and water situation.
>8. Disposition and strength of Fire Fighting Services.
>9. Billets and accommodation available.
>10. Effectiveness of Police and A.R.P. communications.
>11. Which roads are impassable.

" SHUTTLE SERVICE."
>" Exchanging pictures."

WHAT YOU NEED.
>An assistant—phone calls—messages.
>Marking maps—holding the fort.
>Indexed notebooks—celluloid.

Chinagraph pencils—message forms.
Paper fasteners and clips.
Generous supply of maps.
Separate office and telephone.
Log book.

VISITING THE MAYOR.
Treat him with much respect.
"Just after half-past eleven."

HEADS OF DEPARTMENTS.
Friendly relationship with all.
Learn Control Room procedure.
Understand all symbols.

VALUABLE INFORMATION FROM WARDENS.
L.O. should be close to Control Room.
Arranging routes—escorts.
Clearing roads—military traffic.

CHIEF CONSTABLE.
Sometimes Controller.
If not, visit him often.
Police communications good.

LIAISON OFFICER IN BATTLE.
Historic instances of lack of liaison.
Increasing responsibility of Military Commander.
Fighting troops and Civil Defence all look to him.
L.O. then becomes of **great importance.**
L.O.'s mistakes may have tremendous consequences.
"Striving to penetrate the 'FOG OF WAR.'"
Sorting messages.
Do not telephone any but important news.
Summarize rest, and send every hour or so by D.R.
Keep touch with Battalion H.Q.—Mayor—Control.
Chief Constable—Town Clerk—Emergency Committee.
Keep a **log** (Plate 6).
Map—enemy blue, own troops red.
"Keenly striving to pick up information from all sources" (Plate 5).
L.O. not averse to going after information.
Never away for long.
Touch with neighbouring units.
Shuttle service.
Get latest information before going back.

THE L.O.'s RELIEF.
> Must be kept in picture.
> Log book and assistant useful.

DO NOT DO OTHER PEOPLE'S JOBS.

LIAISON OFFICERS WITH MILITARY UNITS.
> Simpler job.
> L.O. to Civil Authorities has been taken as more difficult example.

COMMANDER LIKE A MAN BLINDFOLDED.
> Dependent on other people.

C.O. AND HIS TERRIBLE LOAD.
> Help him!

THE ONE THING HE IS ALWAYS LONGING FOR—QUICK AND ACCURATE INFORMATION. THE ONLY THING WHICH WILL DISPEL THE FOG OF WAR.

INTELLIGENCE AND LIAISON DUTIES

QUITE a number of people seem to confuse the jobs of Intelligence and Liaison, sometimes even to the extent of using the words as though they are interchangeable.

As a matter of fact, the duties are absolutely different; but the personnel carrying them out are naturally brought close together and can be of great mutual help if they are so minded.

" INTELLIGENCE " covers the collection, sorting, checking, registering and accurate presentation of military information. It comes from two Latin words: *inter*=between and *legere*=to choose.

" LIAISON " covers those activities which are necessary to keep two headquarters in close touch with one another's situation, views and actions. It is a French word and apparently means being in close touch with someone else's wife. It is not used in this sense now, but in the less romantic military one.

The personnel engaged in both Intelligence and Liaison have a common object: they are directing all their efforts against that arch-enemy of all operations—

THE FOG OF WAR

In war the commander of any organization or unit has an unenviable job. He may be called upon to make far-reaching decisions affecting the lives of thousands of people. Frequently, although he is short of vital information and may have reason to doubt the accuracy of those reports he *has* received, such is the speed of modern conflict that it would be suicidal to waste time trying to obtain more news, or checking existing reports.

He must decide and ACT.

And if he makes a mistake because he lacks information which COULD have been obtained in time, or because he is ignorant of a neighbouring commander's dispositions or intentions, that would be an avoidable disaster which would NOT have happened had he placed the right men in the Intelligence and Liaison jobs—men who would have acted as the commander's eyes, constantly straining to pierce the dark fog and bring light to his brain.

Now, having shown you how both Intelligence and Liaison personnel have the same objective, *i.e.*, to wage war on that all-pervading fog, we will study them separately, commencing with

THE INTELLIGENCE OFFICER

He should revel in *work*. His Patron Saint should be NOSEY PARKER; his enthusiasm and energy boundless. He should develop the rare gift of being able to separate important from unimportant information. He should regard all people, actions and things with a cold and critical eye, and must be capable of sustained mental effort over long periods. He must have *imagination* to enable him to deduce the enemy's intentions. He must have insight into the inner workings of the human mind. He must be able to foresee what information his commander will ask for and be able to get it in all sorts of ingenious ways. He must have soldierly and systematic habits.

Yes, he must be *some* man!

And even should he possess all these characteristics he will still need assistance from other people in various ways, so he must have the ability to coax, cajole or compel their co-operation.

Having given this description of the exacting standard demanded of the Intelligence Officer personally, let us turn our attention to his responsibilities.

Field Service Regulations say that the basis of all military preparation and plans must be GOOD INFORMATION, and the job of the I.O. is to collect, sort, check, register and present it accurately to his C.O.

Let us take the first—

THE COLLECTION OF INFORMATION

Some I.Os. seem to draw information like a magnet attracting bits of iron, while others collect only a fraction. The explanation is that the former not only encourages people to send information in, but lets them know precisely what kind of intelligence he particularly wants, whereas the latter apparently reasons " It is the duty of these people to send in information and if they don't—well, *I* cannot help it! "

As a matter of fact, you will find everywhere a reluctance to send information in quickly, and there are perfectly astounding cases on record of men keeping most vital information to themselves till too late to be of use.

Some I.Os. are themselves to blame for people hesitating to send in scraps of intelligence: they may at some time have greeted some information with " Oh, that's old! " or " Well, what does that matter? " and this does NOT encourage them to communicate further.

What are the sources from which the I.O. collects his information?

Here they are in diagrammatic form showing the I.O. as the Focal Point of Information from many varied sources (Plate 1).

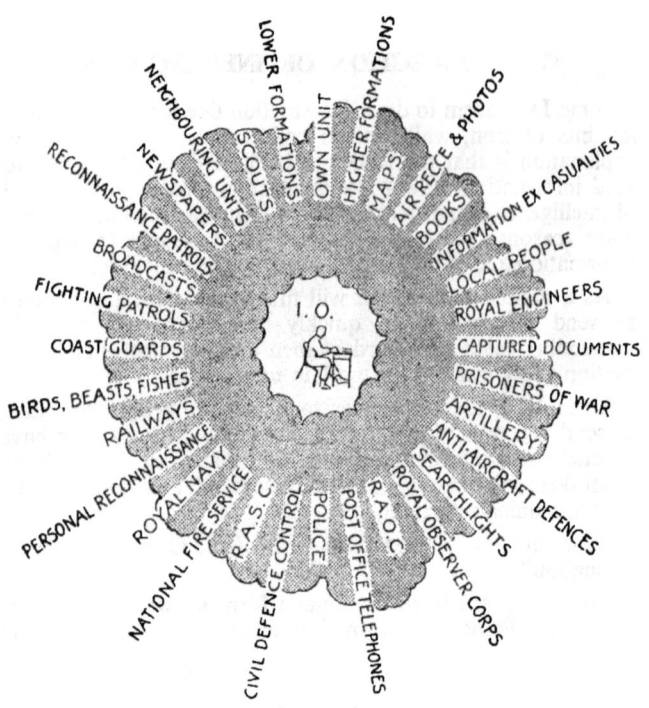

PLATE 1

Here we see the I.O. enveloped in the dense cloud of uncertainty and doubt which takes all the pleasure out of war. Yet, as you will see, he has numerous potential sources of information if he can, by hook or by crook, get hold of it. If only a few of them are able to throw glimmers of light on the situation, all these glimmers put together by an ingenious I.O. will certainly lessen the FOG.

Any one of these sources may be in possession of just that sparkling item of news which would dispel the FOG completely.

Some of these may be useful all the time; others only on occasion, but, when the situation becomes very warlike help in penetrating the FOG may be obtained unexpectedly from any of them.

Let us take in detail some of the most fruitful sources of information.

During battle the most important news is usually sent in by the I.O.'s OWN UNIT. Scouts, reconnaissance patrols, lookout posts, various officers and observers should all the time be sending back information. Frequently a purely negative report is of great value to a commander.

Usually tiny fragments of news come from a number of directions; each in itself may mean very little, but when they are skilfully pieced together they may turn out to be of considerable value.

In " normal " times, before operations commence, the I.O. should consider carefully the specialized training of observers and scouts, also the general training throughout the unit, to ensure intelligent observation, ability to recognize what is of military importance, and quick, clear and accurate reporting.

When things begin to hot up and active operations are imminent, the I.O. should make certain that the important observation posts are manned and that communication with them is as quick and good as it is possible to arrange.

Should there be special points of which the I.O. requires knowledge, they should be notified to all ranks.

A battalion usually has an Intelligence Section of 1 officer and 4 other ranks. Sometimes the I.O. will find it necessary to send out his own scouts to obtain some special item of urgent information.

It will well repay the I.O. to keep in very close touch with his opposite number at the headquarters of HIGHER FORMATIONS. All sorts of news is to be found floating round there, and the I.O. should pay periodic visits with the twofold object of putting the senior I.O. in the picture as regards his own unit and gleaning whatever news is to be had about things generally.

New booklets, intelligence reports, latest details about the German Army, etc., can always be begged, borrowed or stolen during a visit to a Higher Headquarters.

The same applies to visiting NEIGHBOURING and LOWER FORMATIONS (except that it is bad form to steal things from lower formations or neighbours.)

The I.O. should maintain close touch with the NAVY, COASTGUARDS, ENGINEERS, R.A.S.C., R.A.O.C., ARTILLERY, ANTI-AIRCRAFT, SEARCHLIGHT, OBSERVER CORPS and other units which may be stationed in or moving about the area in which the I.O.'s unit operates.

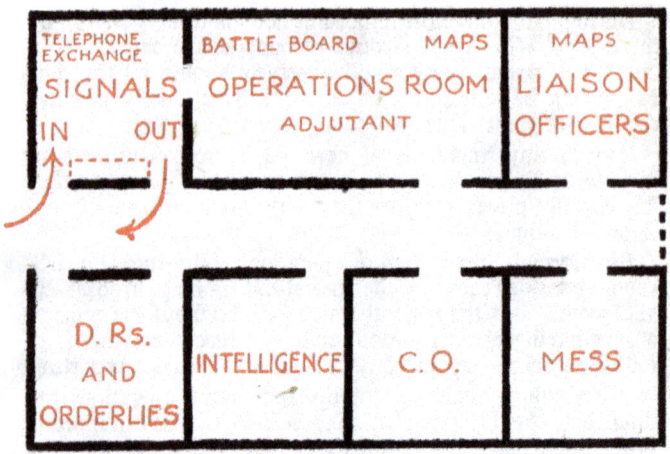

PLATE 2

A BATTALION BATTLE H.Q.

Here you see what you will probably never get—a perfect arrangement for a Battalion Battle H.Q.; but if you note the relative positions of the various rooms you may manage to arrange something near it.

NOTES.

1. *Signals* handy for receiving and sending messages. Separate doors for IN and OUT traffic.

2. *Operations Room* is large with plenty of wall space for battle board and maps. There is room for the Adjutant and his assistants as well as the Intelligence Clerk. There is also a table for the C.O. when he wishes to work there.

3. *C.O.'s Room* is conveniently situated in relation to *Operations Room* and *Intelligence Room*.

4. *Liaison Officers* are quickly available. In their room should be a situation map kept up to date.

5. There is a small Mess where food and rest may be obtained during prolonged operations.

6. *Despatch Riders* and *Orderlies* are quite close.

Certain civil authorities have great facilities for finding out what is going on; for instance, the POLICE, CIVIL DEFENCE CONTROL, POST OFFICE (particularly the TELEPHONES) and the FIRE SERVICE.

RAILWAYS also have very good means of seeing what is happening. They also have first-rate facilities for passing news quickly.

The R.A.F., by reconnaissance and photography, may furnish the answers to a lot of the I.O.'s problems. Under certain circumstances he may even wangle a flight to see for himself. Personal reconnaissance is the best of all, but must be reserved for very special occasions.

Amongst other sources of knowledge are PRISONERS OF WAR and CAPTURED DOCUMENTS, MAPS, BOOKS and LOCAL PEOPLE.

In active operations important information can frequently be obtained from advanced AID POSTS if someone is there who can collect news from wounded men and telephone or send it through to headquarters.

NEWSPAPERS and WIRELESS BROADCASTS must not be overlooked by the I.O., as they are potential sources of supply.

You will note that I have included even the BIRDS, BEASTS and FISHES amongst those who will send the I.O. information. When bodies of men are moving across the landscape lots of feathered and furry scouts are announcing their progress to anyone who is watching the countryside with an understanding eye.

There are, of course, other sources of information and you will discover these for yourselves.

The next point I would emphasize is

LEARN TO SPOT IMPORTANT POINTS

Sometimes in the flood of information coming in during active operations there is a VITAL point, so concealed amongst a lot of unimportant stuff that only an eagle eye and quick mind can detect it.

I will give you an example of what I mean:

Confused fighting had been taking place in the surrounding country and the fog of war hung densely over Battalion H.Q.

A civilian had come in with a strange tale. He had seen a bunch of British soldiers kill several of their own number at a road block and could not understand it. Neither could the I.O.; but the civilian stuck to his story—not only had the British soldiers killed some of their own number, but "they had seemed *pleased* about it!" How did he know that they were pleased? Well, they had *looked* pleased and not only that, had clapped their hands and, what was more, some British soldiers who were just driving up in a lorry had also clapped *their* hands!

"Um, he's nuts! Take him away," said the I.O. and proceeded to consider some messages just received.

Amongst them was one which reported the mysterious loss of a forward position without a shot being fired, and stated that patrols were going out to investigate.

Another message from the same company said that a man who had escaped from the forward position was being sent to Battalion H.Q.

"Where is this man?" said the I.O. "Send him in."

The soldier could not throw much light on the loss of the post; he had been in a dug-out when it happened. He had heard a scream which caused him to run outside. There he had seen four or five of his comrades bleeding on the ground, so he kept on running. No, he did not think they had been shot. Why? Because he had not heard any shots; at least, not exactly. What did he mean by "not exactly"? Well, there *had* been some sounds, but not loud enough for shots. No—it was more like somebody clapping his hands. He could hardly be——

But the I.O. was gone; straight into the C.O.'s room at the double. He had not only solved the mystery but had obtained a piece of intelligence of SUPERLATIVE VALUE. Not only did he know the enemy were attacking our posts dressed as British soldiers, but he knew the signal whereby they IDENTIFIED EACH OTHER!

A few minutes later a party of British troops was rather carefully approaching one of "B" Company's positions. When the leaders got fairly near some of them clapped their hands and immediately a smiling officer stood up and clapped in response. At this the whole party of visitors flocked up to the position and were wiped out by concentrated fire from every weapon the post had got.

Thirty seconds later the officer had stopped clapping but was still smiling, and all over the battle area the vital information was being put to the same good use.

The significance of the clapping would have been lost upon a less astute Intelligence Officer.

In another case, a battalion had been expecting an attack every dawn for weeks, but it had not come and everyone had been lulled into the conclusion that the enemy did not mean to attack at all.

But one night some Germans who had baled out of a bomber barricaded themselves in a house behind our lines and refused to surrender. As all previous "bailees" had readily given themselves up, the I.O. was rather struck by this change of attitude and wondered if some relief had taken place and a different lot of airmen were now being used. Then the *truth* suddenly struck him—the airmen evidently knew an attack was soon to be made and they expected that, if they held out for a few hours, they would be rescued!

The I.O. at once warned his C.O. that attack was imminent and when it came at dawn everyone was absolutely ready to smash it!

I mentioned these two instances to impress how alert the I.O. must be to pounce on the scraps of information which matter and to deduce from them what is likely to happen.

The news which reaches him will be either up-to-date or old, possibly better described as

HOT OR COLD

VERTICAL BATTLE BOARD

UNIT	IN	OUT
SECTOR		
A		
B		
C		
D		
E		
RIGHT		
LEFT		
VARIOUS		

HORIZONTAL BATTLE BOARD

	SECTOR	LEFT	A	B	C	D	E	RIGHT	VARIOUS
IN									
OUT									

PLATE 3

BATTLE BOARDS

Here are two kinds of battle board. If there is sufficient wall space available the horizontal type is best, as the messages are all at a very convenient level for reading. Also several people can study them at one time—a great consideration if there is a rush on.

If there are a lot of units on a vertical battle board the top messages are at considerable height and the bottom messages are difficult to read without stooping right down. Very trying to the short, fat type of C.O.

It is the hot information which is of the greatest importance, and, do not forget, it is going cold rapidly so it must be handled quickly by everybody.

One thick-skulled, unimaginative, dawdling link in the chain along which intelligence has to pass to the C.O. may ruin things by receiving hot, live information, doing nothing with it for a long time, and then passing it on, cold and dead.

The I.O. should look out both above and below himself for such people. They are a menace.

———

It always helps an I.O. in sorting out information if he is very clear in his own mind as to

WHAT HE WANTS TO LEARN ABOUT THE ENEMY

The enemy's *Order of Battle*—his *armament, equipment, distribution* and *organization*. What is his *strength*? Is the *morale* of his troops good? What is his *plan* of attack or defence? Has he any new tactics or new weapons? What kind of shells is he using? Does his target indicate his *intentions*? Where are his *guns*? What about some *counter-battery* work?

The I.O. will probably require information about the tactical features of the country in which operations are taking place. He will also be keenly desirous of learning about the enemy's food and ammunition situation.

Anything bearing on guns, even remotely, is naturally intelligence of the first importance.

Even bacteriological warfare must be kept in mind, as there is no depth of treachery and diabolic villainy to which the Germans will not sink if it appears to suit their purpose, or things begin to get desperate with them.

PLATE 4.

This little Boche has just been captured. In between wars he is a Pferdefleischwurstenschlachtermannsvertreter (*i.e.*, slaughterer-of-horses-for-sausages-assistant) in Hamburg.

Even his wife would not call him a ray of sunshine, but he may be one which shines straight through the fog of war.

Skilfully handled, he may reveal the identity of his unit, the flanking units, the units in reserve. He may spill the beans about the enemy's morale and their casualties in the recent fighting.

He may have observed something, such as movement of guns or tanks, which will give away the enemy commander's plans.

These beady little eyes of his have seen lots of things and vital information may be COAXED, BLUSTERED or SPOOFED out of him by the patient Interrogation Officer whose special job it is.

Incidentally, he should not be allowed to use those same beady eyes in the operations room—the cunning little blighter may succeed in getting away later.

The I.O. should take steps to ensure speedy evacuation of prisoners to where they can be questioned before their morale returns.

No one but the specially trained Interrogation staff should be allowed to talk to them *en route* from capture to the prisoner-of-war cage.

PRESENTING THE PICTURE

Having obtained information from various sources and carefully sorted out the important from the unimportant matters, the I.O. should review the gaps on the picture and initiate whatever steps may be possible to obtain the missing items.

After that he should pass the intelligence to the Adjutant or the C.O. in as clear and concise a form as possible. There should not be a word more than is necessary and the I.O. should carefully avoid any *expression of opinion.*

Nothing is more annoying to a C.O. than intelligence presented in a manner coloured to give weight to somebody else's opinion.

The C.O. wants FACTS *not* OPINIONS.

Later on, should he require it, he will ask the I.O. to express his opinion.

In addition to the C.O., other formations and units will be looking to the I.O. for news and regular situation reports. A comprehensive list of these, with times where applicable, should be prepared in

THE CALM BEFORE THE STORM

so that no one is overlooked in the excitement when things "hot up."

No Intelligence Officer can give a superlative performance in battle unless he has put in a tremendous amount of spadework beforehand, preparing not only himself but all kinds of other people for their very difficult tasks.

By lectures and exercises an energetic I.O. can improve the powers of observation and speed in reporting of every officer and man in the battalion. Very few of them to begin with realize the absolutely vital necessity for passing news quickly, but if the I.O. continually harps on this and in addition gives them a lead as to the *kind* of information required he will be amply rewarded when operations commence.

The training of the Intelligence Section should be a matter

of great pride to the I.O., and their team work in collecting HOT information with terrific speed during actual battle may be a decisive factor.

The I.O. should have a good filing and record system, with Intelligence items classified in a systematic manner so that they can be turned up without the least delay. During operations he must keep a complete LOG BOOK of events.

He should keep up the supply of maps and see that the officers and important N.C.Os. not only have maps in their possession but that they are kept up to date.

All members of the Intelligence Section should be exercised in doing the I.O.'s work so that the temporary absence of the I.O. or even his permanent elevation to loftier spheres will not hinder the flow of information to the C.O.

Such is the speed of modern war that during operations quick information about some specific point may suddenly become vital. In this case the I.O. will dispatch members of the Intelligence Section to obtain it for themselves. Before going out, each man will be told exactly what is required, and if, by previous reconnaissance, he knows which buildings, etc., have a good view of the vital locality and where the nearby telephones are to be found, he has a flying start upon a task which cannot be successful unless it is RAPIDLY carried out.

Sometimes it may be feasible, before operations commence, to divide the battalion area into four parts, giving each member of the Intelligence Section one so that he can make a particular study of it and be prepared with authentic answers should anything happen in his part of the area.

You will doubtless be thinking that the I.O. has a very heavy job. You are right; and on top of his work in acquiring knowledge of the enemy he is expected to know an enormous lot about our own troops, the food, ammunition and morale situation, and so on.

He is also charged with the SECURITY arrangements of the battalion, and has to take steps to counter the activities of spies and fifth columnists, and also to detect and eliminate loose conversations and careless practices amongst our own forces.

He must know the disposition of neighbouring units as well as his own.

Lastly, if he is wise, he will have very secretly made arrangements whereby if the enemy ever occupies the area now held by his battalion certain people in certain places will be able to pass out information about the enemy's numbers and dispositions.

Well, that is an outline of an I.O.'s job. It is a task which calls for HARD WORK, a STOUT HEART and BRAINS.

It is a responsibility which any man may feel extremely proud to carry.

Having dealt with the Intelligence Officer's duties, let us turn to those of

THE LIAISON OFFICER

Although, as has been explained, the L.O.'s job is very different from that of the I.O., there is, none the less, sufficient similarity to warrant the L.O. carefully studying the I.O.'s job and understanding it thoroughly. In what follows I have assumed he has done this.

Liaison Officers are very fashionable nowadays—in fact, they are quite the rage, and consequently tend to be overdone. The result is that officers are being detailed for Liaison duties here, there and everywhere, in places where they are not really necessary.

Now a Liaison Officer, if he is to be a good one, must possess certain characteristics of brain and personality which are not too common, and which make him very useful in other directions within the battalion. Consequently no unit can spare many such officers for Liaison duties, and if they yield to the temptation to send some easygoing nitwit to fill the job great harm may be done and, in the long run, it would have been better had no Liaison Officer been sent at all.

So we will assume that your unit has NOT yielded to temptation but has sacrificed the narrow interests of the battalion in the broader interests of democracy and detailed YOU to do the job of Liaison Officer between your unit and the Civil Defence authorities of the town.

You have not acted as Liaison Officer before. How do you begin?

First of all, consider what information the Mayor, the Police and the A.R.P. Controller will require from you about the military side of operations and get at your fingertips as much of it as is possible before fighting actually begins. Your C.O. will give you a lead as to how much of the information may be passed on to the civil authorities—probably quite a lot of it.

Remember, yours are the eyes through which your C.O. will see the civil side, and it will be through you that the civil authorities will glean most of their knowledge of the military situation.

Whether they get a clear, sharply focused picture or a blurred image depends on YOU!

You must be able to convey to the civil authorities crystal-clear information where necessary about:

1. Military dispositions, situation and headquarters of own and neighbouring units, with telephone numbers, etc.
2. Position of casualty clearing stations, field ambulances, etc.
3. The intention of the Military Commander.
4. The general situation.
5. The progress of the fighting (if any).

This does NOT mean that you will necessarily give all or any of this secret information to the civil authorities; *in fact, you will not divulge a single item unless there is some good reason.*

On the other hand, circumstances may crop up suddenly in which just one or two of the points made known to the suitable authority might be invaluable, so you must know it all.

Periodically when the situation is undergoing change you will go back to your unit to bring your knowledge up to the moment and to convey the civil picture to your battalion.

Some of the things your C.O. may want to know during active operations are:

1. The state of civil morale.
2. A rough estimate of blitz damage.
3. Likelihood of refugee troubles.
4. Whereabouts and capacity of decontamination arrangements.
5. Number of ambulances available.
6. Number of buses in running order.
7. Food and water situation.
8. Disposition and strength of Fire Fighting Services.
9. Billets and accommodation available.
10. Effectiveness of Police and A.R.P. communications.
11. Which roads are impassable through damage.

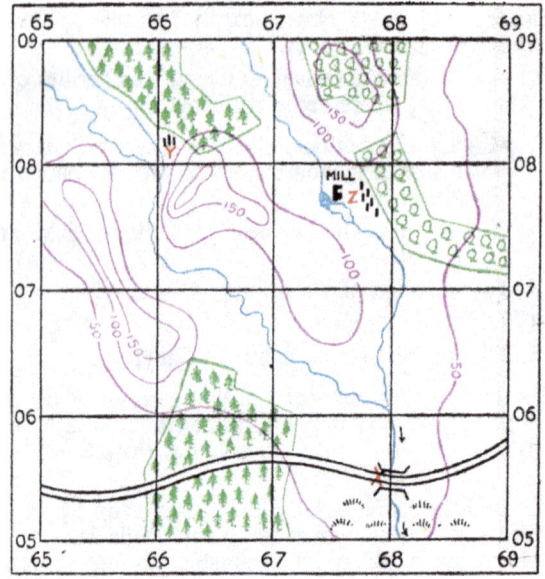

PLATE 5

CHECK YOUR INFORMATION

Scene.—Civil Defence Headquarters.

Time.—During active operations.

MILITARY LIAISON OFFICER (*sees civilian despatch rider walking through room*): "Hi, you there! Where have you come from? UPPER SLUSHTON? . . . Did you see anything on the way? . . . SIX TANKS WITH RED FLAGS ON! . . . Show me on the map. . . . You are CERTAIN they are in this hollow near the wood Y? . . . Where were you when you saw them? . . . On the bridge X. . . . But wait a minute. You could not *see* that hollow from the bridge! Were the tanks close to anything? . . . Haystacks are not shown on maps. . . . Tell me something else. . . . No, potato fields are not shown either. . . . Come, come, my lad! Surely you saw something else as well as the tanks?

... Near the WATER MILL! That fixes them: they are in *this* hollow Z, not *that* one. ... How long ago? Ten minutes. Thanks very much; keep your eyes open when you go back.

"Jones, get Battalion Headquarters quickly!

"Adjutant? Smith speaking. Give me the C.O. ... Yes, it IS important. ... This is Smith speaking, sir. SIX ENEMY TANKS ARE IN HOLLOW 678077. Yes, near the water mill. Twelve minutes ago. ... No, no mistake, sir. ... Yes, I made sure. No, the other road is the better way. Plenty of cover there. ... Yes, I will, sir. ... Very good, sir. ...

"Jones, give me the log. I'll put that in while you are putting them on the map."

———

How easily this Liaison Officer could have passed false information back to his battalion and sent some of his comrades to their deaths! But he was a good fellow and was not content to accept the information without a check.

In all probability the civil authority to whom you are allocated will itself have sent a Liaison Officer to your battalion. Where this is the case, it is wise to start what is called the "SHUTTLE SERVICE," which means that when YOU go back to your headquarters HE comes back to his.

Naturally, you arrange to meet and compare notes at one or other headquarters and to stay at your own headquarters the same length of time so that the two headquarters concerned are not without a Liaison Officer for any longer period than is necessary in exchanging "pictures."

When operations start and the fun waxes fast and furious you will need some help, so, if possible, enlist the aid of a volunteer, or have someone detailed to assist you by dealing with telephone calls, writing or sorting messages, marking maps and "holding the fort" should you be away at any time.

You will need several indexed notebooks, some sheets of celluloid (commonly misnamed "talc") for covering maps, a set of "Chinagraph" pencils for marking dispositions, some message forms, paper fasteners, etc., and a generous supply of maps, both gridded and large-scale.

Persuade the civil authority to give you a separate office and telephone, using, if necessary, the extreme secrecy of your maps, etc., as an argument.

As soon as possible, go to the Mayor's Parlour and introduce yourself. In all your dealings with the Mayor treat him and his opinions with the greatest respect. Visit him fairly frequently. Usually just after half-past eleven in the morning is a good time. If you go any earlier he may think it is "a bit too early to bring it out," which is very disappointing, as it is usually quite a good year.

Get to know as many of the heads of departments as you can, and establish friendly relationship with them all. Go into the Control Room and familiarize yourself with the procedure during a blitz. If you have never seen it you will be astonished. Be sure you understand all the symbols they use on their maps so that you can see the situation at a glance, and do not have to ask for information from some harassed A.R.P. worker when the bombs are falling.

During an attack on the town most valuable information will be sent in by Wardens and others in communication with the Control Room, so that the Liaison Officer should be established as close as possible to it.

A great deal of the L.O.'s work will be with the Controller, such as arranging routes and escorts for mutual support parties which may be sent from outlying districts, clearing roads of refugees and debris to allow military traffic, etc.; consequently, mutual understanding and respect are essential.

Sometimes the A.R.P. Controller is the Chief Constable, and this is very convenient from the L.O.'s standpoint, as it means one contact instead of two.

If, however, the Chief Constable is not the Controller, it will be very necessary to visit him regularly to find out what he knows and to put him in the military picture. His communications are excellent and, at a pinch, he might be able to deliver messages which could not otherwise arrive.

So much for the spadework before operations start. Now for

THE LIAISON OFFICER IN BATTLE

History abounds in the most astonishing instances where friendly or allied forces have been divided and destroyed piecemeal simply because they did not act in unity. The reason for this was that they did not understand one another's dispositions and intentions.

Under certain conditions, invasion for instance, the Military Commander may have continually increasing responsibility thrust upon him until, when danger becomes acute, not only the fighting troops but the Civil Defence Services will all look to him for guidance and control. In this case, the Liaison Officer becomes of great importance, and should he make any mistakes they might be fraught with tremendous consequences.

We will therefore picture a fairly hectic situation in which the town is being blized and the troops defending it are being heavily attacked.

What is the L.O. doing?

LIAISON OFFICER'S LOG

He is striving with all his might to penetrate the FOG OF WAR, to see through its murky depths what is happening, and then to tell the civil authorities and his own C.O.

As messages come in he carefully sorts them out, avoiding congestion on the line by not telephoning any but the really important ones.

The rest of them he summarizes and sends by D.R. every hour or so.

Except for very brief periods during visits to his Battalion H.Q., he is always at the Civil Defence H.Q., at one time in the Control Room, at another with the Chief Constable, and occasionally talking to the Mayor, Town Clerk or Chairman of the Emergency Committee.

He keeps a LOG, in which all happenings of military interest are entered with TIME, SOURCE OF INFORMATION, INCIDENT, ACTION TAKEN and REMARKS.

Also he has a MAP on which the enemy's whereabouts are

PLATE 6

LIAISON OFFICER'S LOG

SHEET Nº.

Nº	DATE	TIME	INCIDENT	REPORTED BY:	ACTION TAKEN
1	69.43	0631	"ALERT"	CONT.	—
2	"	0640	Heavy bombs reported on MARKET Sq. & LOWTOWN District	CONT.	—
3	"	0650	German airman brought in by Police. Unusually truculent attitude	Police	Phoned Bn. I.O at 0655
4	"	0722	Junction HIGH ST - MARKET ST. Blocked by debris.	CONT.	Put on map.
5	"	0743	Enemy occupying SEATON village	BN.	Told Police & Controller
6	"	0745	MAIN ST completely blocked.	N.F.S.	Map
7	"	0803	Civil Defence L.O came back from Bn. H.Q.	—	
8	"	0813	L.O went to Bn. H.Q.	—	
9	"	0819	Telephone fails	—	Borrowed extra D.R.
10	"	0822	Fire spreading along Market Street from Saracens Head towards the Drill Hall	N.F.S.	also 674 Sent to Bn. by D.R.
11	"	0825	L.O. returns from Bn. H.Q.	—	
12	"	0831	Three Enemy Aircraft Machine gun SEATON ROAD	L.O.	Bn. by D.R.
13	"	0910	Telephone in order	Post Office	
14	"	0912	Six Enemy Tanks at 678077.	C.W.D.R.	
15	"	0922	Crowds of Refugees on SOUTH		Telephoned C.O. 0914.

shown in BLUE, and those of our own troops in RED. Other colours show blocked roads, refugees, contaminated areas, and so on.

He is all the time keenly striving to pick up information of all kinds from all sources. Then he sorts it out eagerly in the hope of detecting little gleams of light here and there. These he passes on.

If he urgently needs information and it does not come he is not averse to sallying forth on a bicycle and collecting it for himself, provided it does not take him away from the H.Q. for more than a few minutes.

He knows that at neighbouring units and organizations there are other L.Os. who, if they are kept in close touch, will reciprocate by passing information sideways.

Every now and then, at times agreed with the Civil Defence L.O. at Battalion H.Q., the "Shuttle Service" is put into operation.

Before going back to his Battalion H.Q. the L.O. makes sure that he knows the VERY LATEST situation, both A.R.P. and Police.

He also ascertains if the Controller or Chief Constable has any special points for reference to the Battalion Commander.

When he reaches the headquarters of his battalion he sees the Adjutant or C.O., makes his report, and answers any questions. He is then told the latest news of the military situation, the Battalion Commander's intentions, doubts and fears. Then he visits the Intelligence Officer, is given the latest "low-down," and returns to his civil attachment.

There is, by the way, one other person who must always be kept in the picture—that is the Liaison Officer's RELIEF.

In prolonged operations a relief for the L.O. is absolutely necessary and unless this relief is well posted he may let the whole job down.

Here the LOG BOOK and the volunteer assistant will ensure continuity while the worn-out Liaison Officer takes his hard-earned rest.

Just a word of advice. At Civil H.Q. will be all sorts of people working under great pressure and obviously needing a helping hand. The L.O. has his own job to do, and to do it really well will tax him to the utmost. Therefore, much though he would like to help, he must set his face against taking on any work other than his own.

Now, in conclusion, one important point must be emphasized. It is that the underlying principles of successful liaison are exactly the same, no matter what are the units or organizations concerned.

The preceding example has given an illustration of liaison between a military unit and the civil authorities because it has been found that military officers have more difficulty in effecting liaison with a civil authority than with a military unit; but the task is really the same in both cases.

It has been very truly said that a Military Commander is like a man blindfolded: dependent upon other people for most of the information upon which he has to take far-reaching action.

INTELLIGENCE and LIAISON OFFICERS, do not forget this!

Think of your C.O. and his terrific load of responsibility.

Take a pride in helping him to the very utmost by furnishing him continuously with the one thing he is always longing for—QUICK and ACCURATE INFORMATION, the *only thing* which will dispel the AWFUL FOG OF WAR.

HOW TO MARK UP AN OPERATIONS MAP

1. The map should be covered with celluloid, or "talc" as it is frequently misnamed. The celluloid should be larger than the map by at least two inches all round. There should be white paper under the margins so as to show up any notes written thereon. Marking is done with special greasy crayons called "CHINAGRAPH" which mark easily on the smooth surface.

2. RED is used for *British and Allied dispositions*. BLUE for *enemy*. YELLOW for *gas*.

3. In quickly moving modern warfare, TIMES are most important, and when the enemy is marked at a certain spot it is most important to mark also the time at which he was seen there.

4. When A.F.Vs. or M.T. are to be shown they should be indicated on the side of the road, otherwise they do not show up. An arrow showing which way they were proceeding should be added.

5. If GAS is used WIND DIRECTION and strength (mild —fresh—strong) may be a vital consideration and should be shown on the map.

6. In the margin should be written any information which affects the operations. Times of dawn, sunset and moonrise, and, in districts affected by tides, times of high and low tides.

7. Where there is a MARGINAL NOTE about anything on the map there should be a cross placed close to the sign and the marginal note should be written in the same colour.

8. A circle round a sign usually indicates anti-aircraft and a diamond shows anti-tank; for example:

ARTILLERY   A.A. GUNS   A.T. GUNS

9. Any information which is UNCERTAIN should bear a query.

READING THE OPERATIONS MAP

First look at your watch and you will see that the TIME is now 2000 hrs. What is the SITUATION?

A number of enemy are in FOX COVERT and two MORTARS have just been reported on south side of TRIANGLE WOOD! What does that cross mean?

Oh, a footnote! So they have actually fired on EBB BRIDGE! That looks like business. What have they got behind them? Two machine guns in LONG WOOD, TANKS coming from BLOODFORD direction ten minutes ago and ARTILLERY near FAR COPSE. What have we got to stop those tanks? Nothing on the railway bridge, but a ROAD BLOCK on EBB BRIDGE with an A.T. MINEFIELD covered by two MACHINE GUNS.

Surely that O.P. at CART FARM has ceased to function by now? What says the footnote? Telephoned at 1955 hrs. Stout fellows! They will be useful there. Expect they saw the enemy putting those A.T. mines on the roads near OUTON! And the Boches going into OWL WOOD.

Twenty minutes ago there was a column of INFANTRY on the road past OUTON WOOD going towards SANDYWAY.

There were enemy in OUTON WOOD an hour ago.

MECHANICAL TRANSPORT also going towards SANDYWAY and there was an enemy unit actually there at 1835 hrs.

What's that at HART FARM? Two GERMAN TANKS!

There are a few enemy on the road SANDYWAY—MIDDLETON.

So THAT is all that is known about the enemy. He is probably in a dozen other places not yet reported, but there is enough information to tell us his probable intentions—a typical German " squeeze " from two directions at once.

Will he come along the MAIN ROAD from OUTON?

The use of GAS and the mining of the roads at OUTON (if true!) indicate that he does not intend to use that road.

It looks as if our TANK TRAP at the MARSH will be wasted.

What about moving the A.T. rifles to EBB BRIDGE?

" C " Company is holding the TOWN and has put KNIFE RESTS across the Outon Road and DANNERT WIRE round TOWN WOOD.

No. 13 Platoon is being drawn back to SPARCH WOOD and will be there at 2030 hrs. The wood has WIRE ON STAKES round three sides of it.

" B " Company is approaching from the SOUTH in column of route and there is a section of A.A. guns near PINE WOOD.

Wonder if those A.A. guns can shell those tanks if they come out from HART FARM?

Maybe those tanks are HARBOURING for the night. What a chance for the TANK-HUNTING SECTION! What time does the MOON RISE? Ah, it is on the TALC— 2156 hrs.

That GAS? Why was it put down? Which way is the WIND blowing? That is on the TALC, too. So the GAS was NOT intended to drift to OWL WOOD.

And so we fit together the jig-saw.

TRAINING OF INTELLIGENCE PERSONNEL

As all personnel chosen for " I " duties should be of the most intelligent type it is possible to proceed with their training on the assumption that in the event of casualties any one of them should be capable of stepping into the I.O.'s job and doing it efficiently. Consequently, no distinction need be made between the training of officers and other ranks.

Quite early in their training Intelligence personnel should be given T.E.W.Ts. in which they are called upon to make important decisions upon meagre information. This will impress upon their minds how helpless a Commanding Officer is without information, and will also give them an idea of the type of information needed. The T.E.W.Ts. will lay the foundation of an " INTELLIGENCE " sense, which is rather akin to a good reporter's " NEWS " sense.

Right through the course of training their imaginations should be fired by readings of vivid passages from good books on military history and every new issue of lessons from the various theatres of war should be most carefully studied. Descriptions of authenticated atrocities, well read, serve to make the war a REALITY in their minds, which is the prerequisite of the KEEN INTEREST without which we shall not get the standard of efficiency required.

CURIOSITY regarding the GERMAN ARMY, its ORGANIZATION and its WAYS should be fostered in every possible way. Some of the training films are admirable for this purpose. Personnel taken to see these should be told "You are disguised as a French civilian. You are going to see part of the German Army in action. Report all the INFORMATION you can about their numbers, arms, morale, training, intentions, etc., in writing after you have seen them. Remember, if you are caught you will be SHOT!"

The trainee then sees the film with added interest and observes much more effectively because he is playing a sort of game.

Frequent practice in making all kinds of reports should be given, but starting with *very short ones*. Every report should be gone over with a fine comb for *ambiguities* and *redundancies*. A man receiving his report back with twelve words crossed out without the meaning being affected soon develops a crisp style.

Accuracy is of the utmost importance in these early reports and any doubtful suppositions or incorrect statements should be heavily dropped on.

MAP READING and FIELD SKETCHING are interesting and important subjects. These can be enlivened by TREASURE HUNTS and SPY CHASES over stretches of countryside in which maps, charts and sketches take a large place.

One section of the Intelligence personnel should be used to set the chase for the other, and then vice versa.

All Intelligence personnel should have a working knowledge of communications, including MORSE and practice in R/T. Handling of PIGEONS, etc., SIGNALS procedure, and factors affecting PRIORITY of messages should also be taught and practised.

Other important subjects are SCOUTING and USE OF GROUND AND COVER, ORGANIZATION and USE OF LOOK-OUT POSTS, together with practice in use of FIELD GLASSES, TELESCOPES and NAKED EYES, and the use of the COMPASS and the STARS.

SAND-TABLE exercises are always useful for indoor training.

All personnel should have plenty of practice in MARKING OPERATIONS MAPS, reading MAP REFERENCES, and ENLARGING MAPS.

A very good practice is to take a point on the map and get the whole section to help in constructing the VIEW in a certain direction from that spot, one of the section with artistic ability actually drawing the landscape as the class pictures it to be from the map. Afterwards the section takes the drawing to the spot and compares picture with reality.

"VISUABILITY" is always an entertainment to the section: "Can you see a man here from that spot?"

"Would a tank here be seen by an O.P. in this wood? If not, why not?"

RECOGNITION is a boundless subject. Can you recognize German tanks, infantry, A.F.Vs., planes, personnel, weapons, projectiles, etc.?

SECURITY EXERCISES. Give the section a few sentences, apparently disconnected, overheard in a pub and let them piece the information together. (Do not forget to throw in a spice of irrelevant, pornographic detail. You know the things you overhear in pubs!)

Instruction should be very "snappy"; by that is meant that not too much time should be spent on any one subject, and members of the section should be encouraged to sharpen their wits upon each other by setting problems.

CHECK YOUR INFORMATION

CONVENTIONAL SIGNS
FOR USE ON OPERATIONS MAP

COLOURS
BLUE = ENEMY
RED = BRITISH (AND ALLIES.)
YELLOW = GAS
BLACK = BOUNDARIES
BROWN = ODD NOTES
GREEN = DEMOLITIONS - FLAME TRAPS - MINES

VEHICLES
	SINGLE	COLUMN OF ROUTE
TANKS		
ARMOURED CARS		
MECHANICAL TRANSPORT	o+o	o+o+o+o

HEADQUARTERS
BRIGADE H.Q. .... △
BATTALION H.Q. ....
COMPANY H.Q. .....
PLATOON H.Q. ......

{ INSERT TITLES USING AUTHORISED ABBREVIATIONS

WEAPONS
ARTILLERY ....
DO. ANTI-AIRCRAFT ..
DO. ANTI-TANK ....
MACHINE GUNS ....
MORTARS (STATE SIZE) ..... O M 3"
MINES .... ¤ ¤
MINEFIELD .... ¤ ✧ ¤
                      ¤   ¤
INFANTRY A/T GUNS .....

GAS
MUSTARD
WIND FRESH

OBSTACLES
BARBED WIRE ON POSTS xxxxxxxx
BARBED WIRE COILED ...... ⦿⦿⦿⦿⦿⦿⦿
TANK TRAP .... ◇

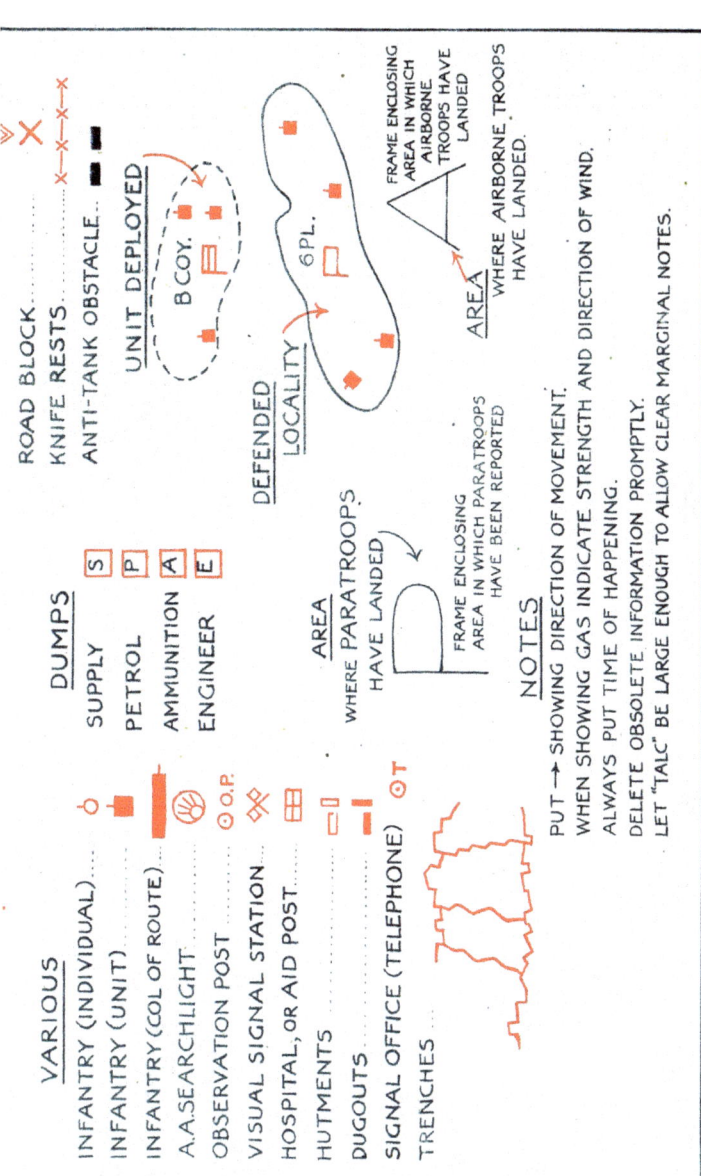

Appendix to "Intelligence and Liaison" published by Gale & Polden Ltd. Aldershot.

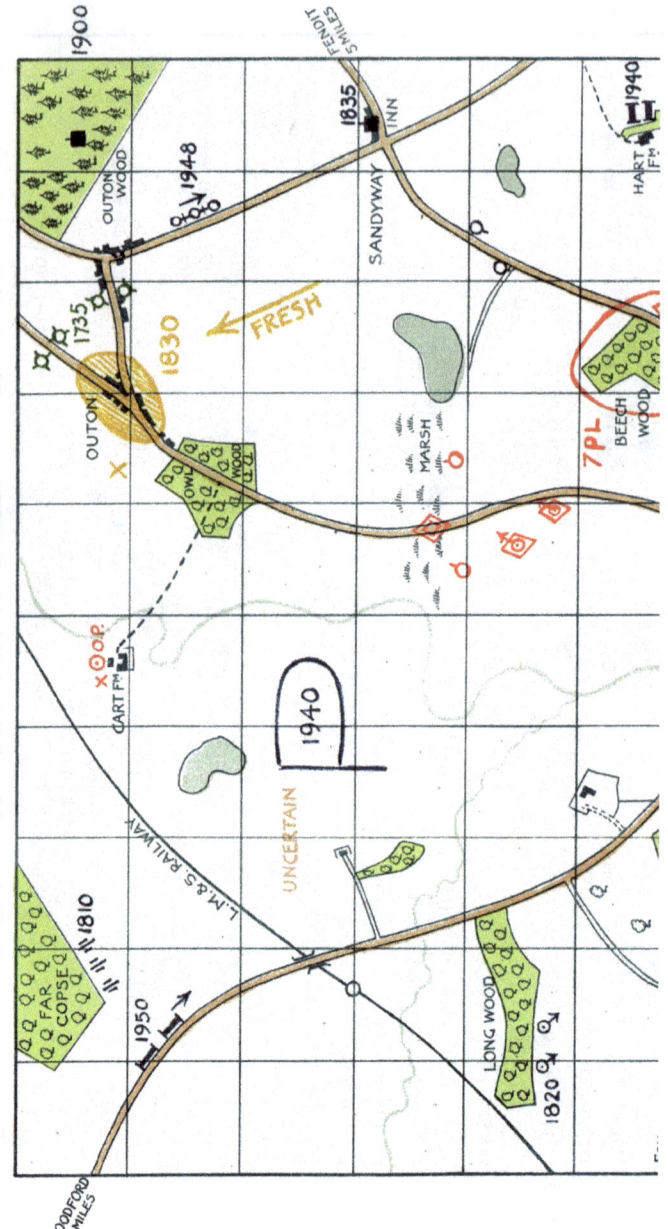

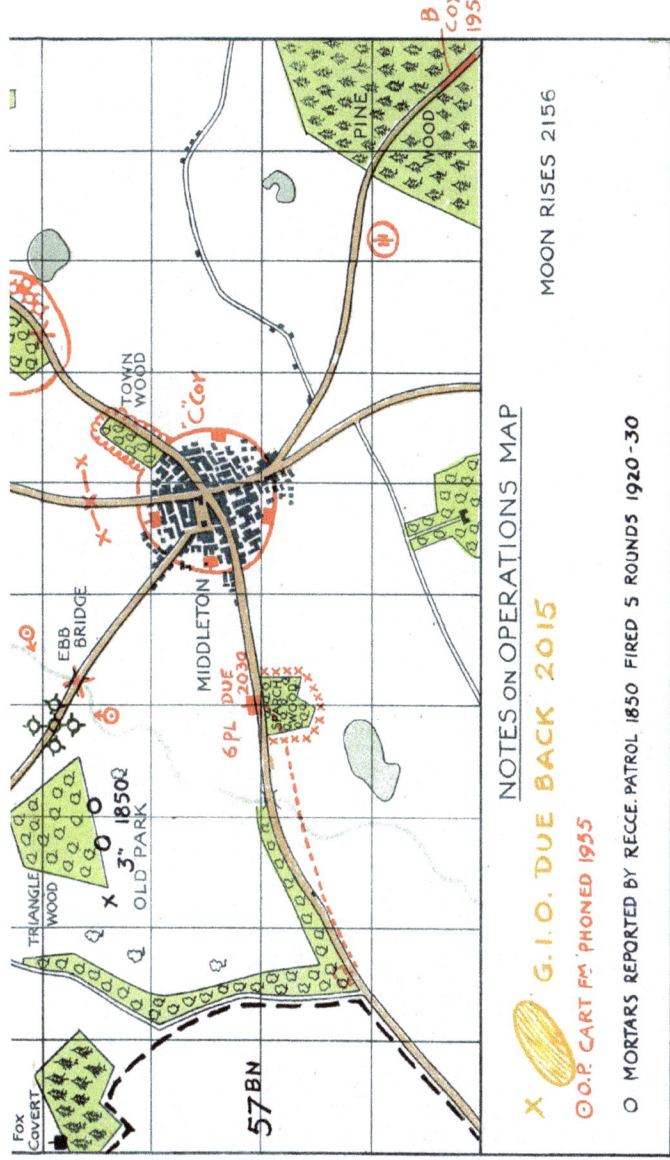

www.ingramcontent.com/pod-product-compliance
Lightning Source LLC
Chambersburg PA
CBHW060225050426
42446CB00013B/3173